FRANCIS FRITH'S

CONWY, DENBIGHSHIRE AND FLINTSHIRE

PHOTOGRAPHIC MEMORIES

PETER THOMPSON was born in South Africa but has lived in Britain for many years. He read History at Aberystwyth and British Vernacular Architecture at Birmingham. He spends his time researching, recording and photographing historic buildings and is dedicated to their appreciation and conservation. He also teaches local history. Peter lives in Barmouth in Gwynedd with his wife Paula and three children where they also run a small hotel in their 17th century farmhouse.

FRANCIS FRITH'S
PHOTOGRAPHIC MEMORIES

CONWY, DENBIGHSHIRE AND FLINTSHIRE

Photographic Memories

PETER THOMPSON

First published in the United Kingdom in 2005 by
The Francis Frith Collection®

Paperback Edition 2005 ISBN 1-85937-826-9
Reprinted in Paperback 2006

Text and Design copyright The Francis Frith Collection®
Photographs copyright The Francis Frith Collection®
except where indicated.

The Frith® photographs and the Frith® logo are reproduced under licence from Heritage
Photographic Resources Ltd,
the owners of the Frith® archive and trademarks.
'The Francis Frith Collection', 'Francis Frith' and 'Frith' are registered trademarks of
Heritage Photographic Resources Ltd.

British Library Cataloguing in Publication Data

Conwy, Denbighshire and Flintshire - Photographic Memories
Peter Thompson
ISBN 1-85937-826-9

The Francis Frith Collection
Frith's Barn, Teffont,
Salisbury, Wiltshire SP3 5QP
Tel: +44 (0) 1722 716 376
Email: info@francisfrith.co.uk
www.francisfrith.com

Printed and bound in Great Britain

Front Cover: LLANDUDNO, *The Parade 1895* 36570t
Frontispiece: PENMAENMAWR, *The Sands 1887* 19909

*The colour-tinting is for illustrative purposes only, and is not intended to be historically
accurate*

Aerial photographs reproduced under licence from
Simmons Aerofilms Limited.
Historical Ordnance Survey maps reproduced under licence from Homecheck.co.uk
Every attempt has been made to contact copyright holders of
illustrative material. We will be happy to give full acknowledgement in future editions
for any items not credited. Any information should be directed to The Francis Frith
Collection.

CONTENTS

FRANCIS FRITH
VICTORIAN PIONEER

FRANCIS FRITH, founder of the world-famous photographic archive, was a complex and multi-talented man. A devout Quaker and a highly successful Victorian businessman, he was philosophical by nature and pioneering in outlook.

By 1855 he had already established a wholesale grocery business in Liverpool, and sold it for the astonishing sum of £200,000, which is the equivalent today of over £15,000,000. Now a very rich man, he was able to indulge his passion for travel. As a child he had pored over travel books written by early explorers, and his fancy and imagination had been stirred by family holidays to the sublime mountain regions of Wales and Scotland. 'What lands of spirit-stirring and enriching scenes and places!' he had written. He was to return to these scenes of grandeur in later years to 'recapture the thousands of vivid and tender memories', but with a different purpose. Now in his thirties, and captivated by the new science of photography, Frith set out on a series of pioneering journeys up the Nile and

to the Near East that occupied him from 1856 until 1860.

INTRIGUE AND EXPLORATION

These far-flung journeys were packed with intrigue and adventure. In his life story, written when he was sixty-three, Frith tells of being held captive by bandits, and of fighting 'an awful midnight battle to the very point of surrender with a deadly pack of hungry, wild dogs'. Wearing flowing Arab costume, Frith arrived at Akaba by camel sixty years before Lawrence of Arabia, where he encountered 'desert princes and rival sheikhs, blazing with jewel-hilted swords'.

He was the first photographer to venture beyond the sixth cataract of the Nile. Africa was still the mysterious 'Dark Continent', and Stanley and Livingstone's historic meeting was a decade into the future. The conditions for picture taking confound belief. He laboured for hours in his wicker dark-room in the sweltering heat of the desert, while the volatile chemicals fizzed dangerously in their trays. Back in London he exhibited his photographs and was 'rapturously cheered' by members of the Royal Society. His reputation as a photographer was made overnight.

VENTURE OF A LIFE-TIME

Characteristically, Frith quickly spotted the opportunity to create a new business as a specialist publisher of photographs. He lived in an era of immense and sometimes violent change.

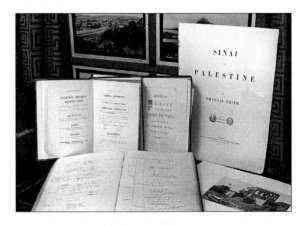

For the poor in the early part of Victoria's reign work was exhausting and the hours long, and people had precious little free time to enjoy themselves. Most had no transport other than a cart or gig at their disposal, and rarely travelled far beyond the boundaries of their own town or village. However, by the 1870s the railways had threaded their way across the country, and Bank Holidays and half-day Saturdays had been made obligatory by Act of Parliament. All of a sudden the working man and his family were able to enjoy days out and see a little more of the world.

With typical business acumen, Francis Frith foresaw that these new tourists would enjoy having souvenirs to commemorate their days out. In 1860 he married Mary Ann Rosling and set out on a new career: his aim was to photograph every city, town and village in Britain. For the next thirty years he travelled the country by train and by pony and trap, producing fine photographs of seaside resorts and beauty spots that were keenly bought by millions of Victorians. These prints were painstakingly pasted into family albums and pored over during the dark nights of winter, rekindling precious memories of summer excursions.

THE RISE OF FRITH & CO

Frith's studio was soon supplying retail shops all over the country. To meet the demand he gathered about him a small team of photographers, and published the work of independent artist-photographers of the calibre of Roger Fenton and Francis Bedford. In order to gain some understanding of the scale of Frith's business one only has to look at the catalogue issued by Frith & Co in 1886: it runs to some 670 pages, listing not only many thousands of views of the British Isles but also many photographs of most European countries, and China, Japan, the USA and Canada - note the sample page shown on page 9 from the hand-written Frith & Co ledgers recording the pictures. By 1890 Frith had created the greatest specialist photographic publishing company in the world, with over 2,000 sales outlets - more than the combined number that Boots and WH Smith have today! The picture on the next page shows the Frith & Co display board at Ingleton in the Yorkshire Dales (left of window). Beautifully constructed with a mahogany frame and gilt inserts, it could display up to a dozen local scenes.

POSTCARD BONANZA

The ever-popular holiday postcard we know today took many years to develop. In 1870 the Post Office issued the first plain cards, with a pre-printed stamp on one face. In 1894 they allowed other publishers' cards to be sent through the mail with an attached adhesive halfpenny stamp. Demand grew rapidly, and in 1895 a new size of postcard was permitted called the court card, but there was little room for illustration. In 1899, a year after Frith's death, a new card measuring 5.5 x 3.5 inches became the standard format, but it was not until 1902 that the divided back came into being, so that the address and message could be on one face and a full-size illustration on the other. Frith & Co were in the vanguard of postcard development: Frith's sons Eustace and Cyril continued their father's monumental task, expanding the number of views offered to the public and recording more and more places

5			+	
6	St Catherine's College		+	
7	Senate House & Library		+	
8			+	
30	Gerrard Hostel Bridge		+	+	+	+
0	Geological Museum		+	
1	Addenbrooke's Hospital		+	
2	St Mary's Church		+	
3	Fitzwilliam Museum, Pitt Press &c		+	
4			+	
5	Buxton, The Crescent		+
6	The Colonnade		+
7	Public Gardens		+
8			+
9	Haddon Hall, View from the Terrace		+
40	Millers Dale		+

in Britain, as the coasts and countryside were opened up to mass travel.

Francis Frith had died in 1898 at his villa in Cannes, his great project still growing. The archive he created continued in business for another seventy years. By 1970 it contained over a third of a million pictures showing 7,000 British towns and villages.

FRANCIS FRITH'S LEGACY

Frith's legacy to us today is of immense significance and value, for the magnificent archive of evocative photographs he created provides a unique record of change in the cities, towns and villages throughout Britain over a century and more. Frith and his fellow studio photographers revisited locations many times down the years to update their views, compiling for us an enthralling and colourful pageant of British life and character.

We are fortunate that Frith was dedicated to recording the minutiae of everyday life. For it is this sheer wealth of visual data, the painstaking chronicle of changes in dress, transport, street layouts, buildings, housing, engineering and landscape that captivates us so much today. His remarkable images offer us a powerful link with the past and with the lives of our ancestors.

THE VALUE OF THE ARCHIVE TODAY

Computers have now made it possible for Frith's many thousands of images to be accessed almost instantly. Frith's images are increasingly used as visual resources, by social historians, by researchers into genealogy and ancestry, by architects and town planners, and by teachers involved in local history projects.

In addition, the archive offers every one of us an opportunity to examine the places where we and our families have lived and worked down the years. Highly successful in Frith's own era, the archive is now, a century and more on, entering a new phase of popularity. Historians consider the Francis Frith Collection to be of prime national importance. It is the only archive of its kind remaining in private ownership. Francis Frith's archive is now housed in an historic timber barn in the beautiful village of Teffont in Wiltshire. Its founder would not recognize the archive office as it is today. In place of the many thousands of dusty boxes containing glass plate negatives and an all-pervading odour of photographic chemicals, there are now ranks of computer screens. He would be amazed to watch his images travelling round the world at unimaginable speeds through internet lines.

The archive's future is both bright and exciting. Francis Frith, with his unshakeable belief in making photographs available to the greatest number of people, would undoubtedly approve of what is being done today with his lifetime's work. His photographs depicting our shared past are now bringing pleasure and enlightenment to millions around the world a century and more after his death.

CONWY, DENBIGHSHIRE AND FLINTSHIRE
AN INTRODUCTION

THIS BOOK covers the three new counties of Conwy, Denbighshire and Flintshire, much of which was in the county of Clwyd until 1996. Generally, the three counties are distinguished by a number of mountain ridges and fertile valleys, running north to south. These mountains and valleys are always North Wales' greatest attraction and have always been their greatest defence. The terrain has certainly determined the development of the region, both culturally and economically.

When we approach and cross the river Dee and enter Wales, it may take a few miles before we realise that we have entered a different country. It may be the place names and the bilingual signs at first that tell us, but the hills of the hinterland of Flintshire, Denbighshire and Conwy confirm that we are in a different country. It is quite obvious that the language of the Celts is vital to this nation, and the few English place names are merely a later overlay to the history that persists beneath them.

CONWY *1898* 42386

This history is the stuff of romance, of myths and legends, of heroism and some tragedy. But it is more than this that makes this area unique. We can see in the architecture, the small villages and, of course, the changing landscapes as we move further into the Welsh heartlands that this part of Wales is very distinctive. It has been inhabited by prehistoric man, and invading Romans. Saxons and Normans have all laid their claims on the products of its soil. Here too Edward I began building his ring of great castles to subdue Wales. Industry has extracted what it wanted over the last 200 years. But now the future seems to be tourism and continuing agriculture in its fertile hills and valleys: a much quieter prospect.

Conwy is the largest county featured in this book, and extends to within sight of Snowdon itself. It is divided from Conwy in the north to Betwys-y-Coed in the south by the beautiful Vale of Conwy with some of the most spectacular scenery in the region. From Llanfairfechan to Kinmel Bay the coastal strip has been a draw for tourists for several hundred years, and the medieval walled town of Conwy, the Victorian planned town of Llandudno, and Colwyn Bay now spar with each other for trade.

But before the road was laid along the north coast the route and the road made for an arduous journey. The trail around Penmaenmawr left virtually no room between waves and mountain. Macaulay noted that in 1685 a viceroy making for Ireland via Holyhead took five hours to travel from St Asaph to Conwy. Between Conwy and Beaumaris he had to walk a great part of the way, and his lady was carried in a litter. His carriage was carried 'entire' after him - it was usual to dismantle carriages at Conwy

and carry them to the Menai Straits!

Denbighshire enjoys only a short strip of the North Wales 'Riviera' with Rhyl and Prestatyn as its representatives, but it offers much more inland. At Rhuddlan, Edward I passed his Statute of Rhuddlan in 1284; this led to Wales being divided into shires, as in England, and brought administratively to heel (or so he thought). Extending southwards from the ancient cathedral city of St Asaph, the Vale of Clwyd is recognised as one of the most fertile and compelling of Welsh heartlands, and here the early towns of Denbigh and Ruthin have seen great conflict between the Welsh and the English down the centuries. This is the homeland of Owain Glyndwr, a marcher lord who rose against the English in 1400 and fought heroically for nine years to shed the yoke of their rule before succumbing to Henry V in 1409. Yet the embers of his memory still persist centuries later.

During the early years of success for Glyndwr, towns like Ruthin and Denbigh and St Asaph and then the whole of Wales fell to his sword. Calamities did not stop. Jasper Tudor, supporter of the future Henry VII, landed an army near Barmouth in Merioneth during the Wars of the Roses, led them to Denbigh, and sacked part of the town. The Civil War saw an eleven-week siege of the castle at Ruthin before it fell to General Mytton in 1645. Nowadays the weekly markets may be as much excitement as some people see. The gentle trade of glove making was Denbigh's most famous industry, and tourists may seek clues to earlier activity in these attractive towns. The medieval timber-framed buildings in Ruthin are especially attractive.

The 16th century saw two monumental efforts to inspire the survival of the Welsh language: William Salisbury of Dolbelydr near St Asaph produced a grammar of Welsh, and William Morgan of St Asaph set about translating the Bible into Welsh. This single act ensured its survival as a living language.

Flintshire borders England, and the Deeside region juxtaposes industry with rural delight. The coastal strip includes Queensferry, Connah's Quay, Shotton and Flint, which have been highly productive industrial powerhouses for Britain in the production of steel, paper, cotton, bricks and tiles, and extracted minerals; but these industries are in decline or have vanished now. Today the area is boosted by EU-funded regeneration initiatives. Just over the border, in Wrexham, coalfields contributed to this 'industrial north' of Wales. Now the vestiges of these industries serve as heritage centres for tourists.

Holywell is unique. It is most famous for St Winifride's Well, said to date from a Celtic foundation, but it was the Romans who first recorded a spring here; it has been such a popular place of pilgrimage that it has been named 'the Lourdes of Wales'. The town, nevertheless, grew on 18th-century industry, producing cotton and paper.

Further south, the market town of Mold, founded by William Rufus in c1100, enjoyed medieval prosperity, but it is now a somewhat sleepy market town and administrative centre for the county. Hawarden is famously known for its greatest resident, William Gladstone, and his presence is still felt in the buildings and books he left not only to the town but to the nation.

Further away from the Dee, the foothills begin to rise up to the ridge of the Clwydian Range along which the Offa's Dyke Path now runs. The ridge summits are occupied by the remnants of Iron Age hill forts, but the archaeology of the dyke itself is found some way to the south near Treuddyn in the south of Flintshire. The dyke was a tremendous achievement of civil engineering that stretched from sea to sea. It was begun around AD 760 by King Offa, and was probably constructed to be a defensive boundary between Mercia and the Welsh kingdoms. On these gentle slopes will be found numerous small hamlets connected by twisting lanes hardly more busy than they were 200 years before, and seemingly untouched by the passing of time or the intrusions of industry and commerce.

More recently, as we move into the years of the Industrial Revolution, the story of these counties reveals man's efforts to tame the landscape. Modern road building and innovative engineering was undertaken by the likes of Robert Stephenson, Telford, and Brunel; they overcame great physical barriers as they improved communications through to Ireland and sought more efficient ways of transporting the stone, coal, slate and other materials out of North Wales. The railway also laid the foundation for

LLANRWST, *Gwydyr Castle 1895* 36914

the influx of the leisured classes. The railway, from the mid 19th century onwards, spread its tentacles ever wider, bringing ever-increasing numbers of visitors in, and further in to the mountains and valleys.

In the 20th century, with the motor car becoming available to more and more people, we witness a change in the way visitors travelled to Wales, particularly after World War II. Of course, the local population also took advantage of this great 'liberator' - and yet still the hinterlands that we see in these photographs reveal little change. Perhaps only the North Wales coast and the industrial areas we have discussed have altered and grown to any marked degree.

The pictures that follow reveal many aspects of how people lived and worked in these counties and the effects that leisure had on the economy and the built environment. Some of the earliest photographs show Victorians at work and going about their daily business, and we see a quite different way of life. We see the Victorians at play too as we view holidaymakers enjoying the sun in their voluminous dark clothes - they must have been hot! Shops displayed their goods outside in ways that would upset the health inspector today. In later pictures we see fashions changing and becoming less formal, and the post-World War II views bring increasing numbers of motor cars, holidaymakers and light summer dresses and ways of living that are within the living memory of many people today.

The highly skilled photographers employed by Francis Frith have managed to capture much of these later changes. It is interesting to note that in the early Victorian images the scene is often filled with people deliberately posing for the camera. As time moves on, the photographs become more objective as photography becomes less and less of a novelty, and we can witness this subtle change. Enjoy poring over these images; they may well stimulate some interesting memories.

BETWYS-Y-COED, *The River c1876* 8580

FLINTSHIRE - HAWARDEN, HOLYWELL AND GRONANT

HAWARDEN
Hawarden Castle, the West Front 1888 20646

This was the marital home of William Gladstone, the Prime Minister. The castle has had several facelifts, the latest being when Sir Stephen Richard Glynne enlarged and re-fronted the building and gave it its present name in 1810. As we moved into the modern age, the labour intensive gardens were later turfed over, a sad loss.

◄ **HAWARDEN**
The Old Castle 1888
20649

The path beckons the visitor to venture into the woods to discover the story that this castle might tell. The large keep peers over the trees in a show of strength, but the castle was mostly in ruins when this photograph was taken, and the gardens were as much the attraction to visitors as the castle was.

◄ HAWARDEN
The Village 1903 49656

Noted for being the home of William Gladstone, who is commemorated by the water fountain on the right, Hawarden has a long history. The scene here is little altered today. The curious row of arches beyond the hotel are said to be the site of the medieval shambles or shops, and some are now converted to a bus shelter. The horses and carriage perhaps wait for visitors from the entrance to the old castle.

◄ HAWARDEN
St Deiniol's Library, Hostel and Church 1903 49661

William Gladstone laid the foundation stone for this impressive building in 1899 and donated his library of 250,000 books; after his death his family built a further wing in 1906, to the right of the porch block, to provide accommodation for resident students. It still thrives today as a place for reflective study, and ensures that Gladstone's legacy continues.

▼ **QUEENSFERRY,** *The Bridge c1960* Q10031

This is the old Queen Victoria Jubilee Bridge. A steel bascule bridge, a portion of the bridge rose upwards, to make a clear path for shipping. Notice the wooden cages around the pillars of the bridge.

► **QUEENSFERRY**
The Roundabout c1960 Q10025

The road leading to the Dee estuary is relatively peaceful in 1960, and the roundabout, resplendent with flower beds, is a reminder of earlier civic pride in such innovations. There are places to park too, and shops to visit. Today the roundabout has gone, and a new traffic scheme has devoured much of the foreground.

◀ **QUEENSFERRY**
The Chapel c1960
Q10027

This slightly unusual church, with clerestory windows, is now known as the church of the Blessed Trinity. The van is delivering Cerebos Salt, whose dark blue and white livery was a common sight well into the 1960s.

▶ **CAERGWRLE**
Castle Street 1939
C363040c

This quiet street scene belies the tumultuous events unfolding in the wider world. A headline on a newspaper placard reads: 'Russia's terms to Britain', referring to Russia's desire to create a formal alliance against Nazi Germany. The failure to do so inevitably quickened the road to war, but it is doubtful that even that would have disturbed the scene we see here.

► **SHOTTON**
The John Summers Works and the Dee c1965 S429006

The production of steel was reaching the end of its competitive life by the time of this photograph, and within a couple of decades the industry was to be transformed - and greatly reduced. This bleak photograph has a certain pathos now. In its heyday, 13,000 men were employed at Shotton; but in 1980, 6,000 jobs were lost. The effects on Shotton and Deeside were devastating as the decline of the steel industry continued. The modern Corbis Steelworks now only employs about 700 men. In 1895, the Summers family had bought 40 acres of reclaimed marshland for £5. By 1909 the site had grown from 40 acres to 10,000 acres of marshland. The intervening years tell the story, and reveal the tribulations of a community.

◄ CONNAH'S QUAY
The Civic Centre c1965
C370003

The Civic Centre in Connah's Quay, one of several buildings laid out as a formal civic area, was began in 1960, with the stone being laid by the steel magnate John F Summers; the Summers family, while benefiting immensely from the production of steel, were also great benefactors in this area. These buildings, along with a library and others, form a self-conscious expression of municipal pride that was common with the advent of the 1960s.

▶ **HALKYN**
The Castle c1955
H286009

This 1820s structure, built by the Grosvenor family, required the remodelling of the old nuclear village of Halkyn, including its church, to accommodate it. The influx of population into the area that came with the growth of the mining industry from the late 18th century and the demands for ostentatious houses by the new landowners caused considerable strife with the old farmers and commoners, who saw their rights and livelihoods diminishing with the enclosure of common land.

◀ **PENTRE HALKYN**
The Square c1955
P198005

'The Square' seems rather a grand name for this scene. Only the central rump of this row of cottages survives today in the village, and is barely recognizable from the photograph. A large number of these small cottages have been 'done up', and not always to their advantage, but the alterations do reveal a changing pattern in village life.

▲ **MOCHDRE,** *General View c1960* M200011

New housing developments are suggestive of more to come, which they certainly did. The passenger train leaves a plume of steam behind it, an emblem of the changes that were about to happen; this rural landscape was soon to be altered beyond recognition.

◀ **MOLD**
The Junction, the Bridge and the Sheds 1904 55292

Apart from the ones in the sheds, this scene is uncluttered by carriage or locomotive, and gives a somewhat ghostly and atmospheric impression. It must have affected the photographer enough to record it. At this time the train was the main means of transporting people any distance.

MOLD
Wrexham Road c1955
M201007

That Mold has prospered
can be seen in the variety
expressed in its built fabric.
Here there are medieval
buildings concealed by
more recent frontages,
along with Georgian and
Victorian buildings and the
later mock-Tudor building
on the right - all display a
healthy economic history.

▲ **MOLD,** *High Street c1955* M201006

This is a splendid county town; we see awnings shooting over the shop fronts and a number of cars dotting the kerbs. Bicycles propped up against the curbs predate modern bike racks. On the right is a branch of Hepworths, whose shop sign declares it to be a 'clothiers' rather than the 'tailors' they were later to become. The tower of St Mary's Church overlooks the town.

▲ **MOLD,** *The Last Half Mile to Moel Fammau c1960* M201056

Moel Fammau is the highest peak in the Clwydian Range. On its summit are the remains of Jubilee Tower, built at a cost of £6,000 to celebrate the Jubilee (the 50th year of his reign) of George III in 1810, and once a prominent landmark. The tower was 150 feet high and 60 feet in diameter, and constructed in the Egyptian style. The tower was still being finished in 1816; it was never quite completed, and it fell down in 1862.

▲ **FLINT,** *The Castle c1955* F120038

The reduction of this castle of Edward I, built in around 1275, was thorough. The chimney stacks behind speak of a different kind of power, that of industry.

27

FLINT
Trelawney Square
c1955 F120017

The monuments to the fallen seen here have been relocated elsewhere in the town. Oldfellows Hall is on the left. On the right is T H Pumphrey, a general hardware business established in the 19th century. The business moved into car and bicycle hire in the 20th century, but by the 1960s the shop had fallen into disuse. In 1969 it was demolished and the monuments were moved to make way for the new road that now dominates this scene.

▼ **FLINT,** *Church Street c1950* F120018

It was 1938 when Gary Cooper starred in 'The Adventures of Marco Polo', showing in Flint in the Grand cinema.

► **FLINT**
General View c1950
F120022

This view down into Flint is noteworthy for a number of reasons. We can see the heavy industrial scene, the chimney stacks and the Courtaulds building in the distance (left). A good deal of the old Flint still seems to be in place - in the 1960s there was some rebuilding, now so prominent from this viewpoint. The cattle being driven towards the silhouetted industrial buildings seem to signify a vanishing, rustic way of life.

◄ FLINT MOUNTAIN
The Village 1936
F212007

There does not appear to be much here that a blink of the eye would not miss, yet postcards depicted Flint Mountain as a place to stop and visit during these years. A lone Austin makes its way towards the camera, mindful of the horse and cart unloading.

► CILCAIN
The Village Square c1955 C367038

The White Horse Inn (facing us, left) is now the last of seven public houses that are said to have once traded in the village; it is remarkable that the local population of so many small Welsh villages like this could support so many hostelries. The great movement of labour away from agriculture and related trades has had a disastrous effect on the viability of what was often the hub of village life.

RHOSESMOR
The Pond c1955
R285004

Here we see an image of disappearing Britain: the village pond, many of which have been removed since the time of this photograph, with a backdrop of cottages. These date from different periods, and those on the right show successive and ever lower extensions. Original Georgian and Victorian sash windows help the buildings to retain their individual character - this was before the introduction of UPVc.

NANNERCH, *Celtic Crafts c1965* N111028

As the motor car became the prime mode of transport after the war, every small village and town sought to capitalize on the additional, but highly seasonal, trade it brought. This shop sold knitwear and pottery; the shop name is directed at a tourist market, and the coracle outside the pottery is a further 'prop' to entice customers. It has not lasted. Beeching closed the railway line, and the village has been bypassed by the A541; the modern village website proclaims that 'there are no shops in Nannerch'.

HOLYWELL, *The Bath, St Winifride's Well c1930* H522001

Dating from the 7th century, and named after Winifride, or Gwenffrewi in Welsh, the holy well has been the site of pilgrimage ever since, and known as 'the Lourdes of Wales'. The waters are said to have amazing restorative powers, and Henry V came here to pray in 1415 before the Battle of Agincourt. The visitors here are probably not pilgrims, but merely appreciating one of the 'Seven Wonders of Wales'.

▼ **HOLYWELL,** *Relics at St Winifride's Well c1930* H522065

These relics, the crutches not required by those fortunate enough to be freed from disability by the curative powers of the well's water, act as reminders to those who might doubt the profound source of the healing.

► **HOLYWELL**
The Caves at Holway c1930 H522068

These impressive caves, their interiors hewn out of the limestone rock, were later to be used to house the wartime 'bouncing bomb'.

◀ **HOLYWELL**
Basingwerk Abbey after its Restoration c1930
H522091

The keeper poses somewhat nervously for the camera amidst the ruins of this Cistercian abbey founded around 1132. Most of the remains date from the 13th century. Much of the stone was taken by the predatory new landed classes following the Dissolution of the Monasteries by Henry VIII.

▶ **HOLYWELL**
St Winifride's Well c1930 H522116

This fine collection of medieval buildings was rebuilt in around 1490 by Margaret Beaufort. The well in their centre has been the objective of pilgrimages for centuries; pilgrimages here have been recorded since 1115, and have been made regularly since.

HOLYWELL
High Street c1960
H522136

Much of the prosperity of the town derived from the nearby Greenfield Valley. The cotton mill and the later factories were in full production from the 18th century, but now they form part of a heritage park for tourists. A young mother ambles down the middle of the street behind a pram, while a policeman converses with a passer-by.

▶ **HOLYWELL**
High Street c1960
H522141

Before the advent of the car moved shoppers to out-of-town stores, main streets such as this displayed a rich multiplicity of goods, with regional shops trading beside the more well-known nationals like Woolworth's and Dewhurst the butcher's (left). It is interesting to note that some of the shop fronts have been modernised with the new fashion of plain sheet glass windows, a process that is now going full circle with the re-insertion of 'traditional Victorian' shop fronts.

◀ **LLOC**
The Singing Kettle c1950 L248011

The jaunty hanging kettle optimistically beckons visitors to a Swiss-style establishment that must belie a Wales only just awakening from its post-war austerity.

▲ **BRYNFFORDD,** *The Village c1965* B463007

The 1950s and 1960s were ideal decades for taking to the quiet country roads and villages to enjoy the exhilaration of motor-car driving. The motorists may not have known as they drove through the sleepy village that the church at Brynffordd reveals an interesting story. A church had been built by the local landowners at nearby Panatasaph, but the family converted to Catholicism. A bitter dispute followed, but the Bishop of St Asaph had to relinquish the church. Funds were raised, and St Michael's Church was built in Brynffordd in 1853.

◀ **PANTASAPH**
*The Road to the Village
c1940* P193057

As the farmer leads his two draught horses along the road, the Convent of St Clare can be seen in the background. Pantasaph was known for the large number of Roman Catholic institutions built in and around the village.

PANTASAPH
St Clare's Convent
c1940 P193059

A sombre and rather depressing view of this large and complex set of 19th-century buildings mirrors the sad decline in its fortunes - falling numbers led it into disuse. Five hundred orphan children once lived within its care.

It is now being rehabilitated and redeveloped, and commercial pragmatism has swayed the local authority in its favour after a 12-year battle with local groups who sought to retain its spiritual and architectural identity.

WHITFORD, *The Church c1915* W642024

Whitford church, dedicated to St Mary and St Beuno, is just over 5 miles to the south east of Prestatyn. It is Perpendicular in style, though little architectural detail survives from the late medieval period. While the church was largely rebuilt in the 1840s, the arcade and north aisle roof are 16th-century.

GRONANT
Llanasa Road c1955
G167016

A village inn, the 1930s car, and the shop all seem to have a timeless feel to them; they stand undisturbed on the outskirts of Prestatyn. Even today this end of the small village is remarkably peaceful.

GRONANT
The Post Office c1955 G167076

At the other end of the extended village of Gronant, before the area was given over to holiday accommodation and caravans, the post office not only sold stamps but also petrol and paraffin.

GRONANT
The Village c1965 G167132

This picture of the village is typical of rural Wales in the 1960s. A small number of houses still manages to support a pub and grocery store - this one is part of the Mace chain. Gifts are also offered to those that venture up from the caravans at the 'other' Gronant lower down the hill.

THE VALE OF LLANGOLLEN AND THE SOUTH

LLANGOLLEN
Castell Dinas Bran 1913 65824A

Perched above Llangollen, this ancient fortification, whose name translates roughly as 'castle of the fort of the crow', dates from the Iron Age; medieval fortifications were added later, possibly in the 13th century. It has proved an unmissable attraction for visitors to the town for hundreds of years.

LLANGOLLEN
On the Canal 1913
65830

Llangollen has been a magnetic location since the 19th century. One of its principal attractions has been its canal, especially where it spans the Dee using Thomas Telford's marvellous 121ft-high Froncysyllte Aqueduct, built in 1805. Here we see a horse leading a somewhat empty pleasure boat towards the aqueduct for what can be an unnerving experience.

LLANGOLLEN, *The Bridge c1965* L76146

The town is most famous now for its annual international eisteddfod, one of the high spots of the cultural calendar in Wales. Most of the year it exists as a busy town on the A5; it has always attracted a great number of visitors, many of them water sports enthusiasts who have come to the River Dee. Today, the bridge here is often thronged with people watching the canoeists below. Perhaps the people on the bridge in this scene are looking at some earlier paddlers.

▲ LLANRHAEADR YM MOCHNANT
The Square c1955 L246006

The small village is famous for its waterfall and for being the home of William Morgan, vicar of Llanrhaeadr and 16th-century translator of the Bible into Welsh. Here we see a fine old 1930s car gracing the square. It is remarkable that today this scene is almost identical, with almost every physical detail unaltered. Not unlike other locations, the village has an identity problem. It has belonged to Denbighshire, Flintshire and Clwyd, but it has recently been nudged out into Powys.

▶ *detail of L246006*

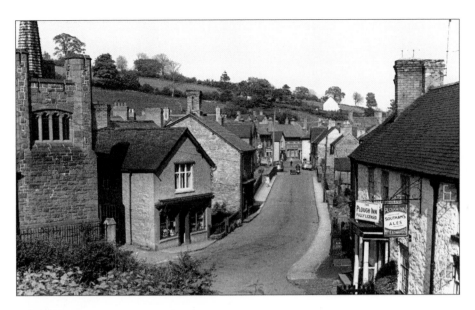

LLANRHAEADR YM MOCHNANT
The Village c1955
L246050

We are looking eastward towards the Square. This village's spells in various counties have not affected its charming identity. It is very much set in its rural isolation with visitors just passing through or making their way to the famous waterfall nearby, Pistyll y Rhaeadr.

GLYNDYFRDWY, *The Post Office c1955* G165001

This photograph appears to show a quiet village where nothing much happens apart from an amble down to the post office to buy a few stamps. However, near here at his manor of Glyndyfrdwy, Owain Glyndwr proclaimed himself Prince of Wales on 16 September 1400, so beginning his 9-year rebellion against English rule.

◄ **CARROG**
The Bridge c1960
C364035

Cattle near the water
suggest a hot summer's
day in the village of
Carrog. The fine stone
bridge of 1661 has
yet to experience the
heavy traffic of more
recent times. Carrog,
or Llansantffraid
Glyndyfrdwy, is in the
heart of the lands of
Owain Glyndwr, the
marcher lord.

◄ **CARROG,** *The Church 1888* 20772

The church was built in 1611 to replace one that had been washed away by a great flood in 1601.
It was also extensively repaired in 1864, about twenty years before this photograph was taken.

▲ **CORWEN,** *The Village c1940* C371003

Dedicated to two 6th-century saints, St Mael and St Sulien, this church looks down on the town and has done since
medieval times. Early references to the church and the number of clerics suggest it was a mother church to the area.

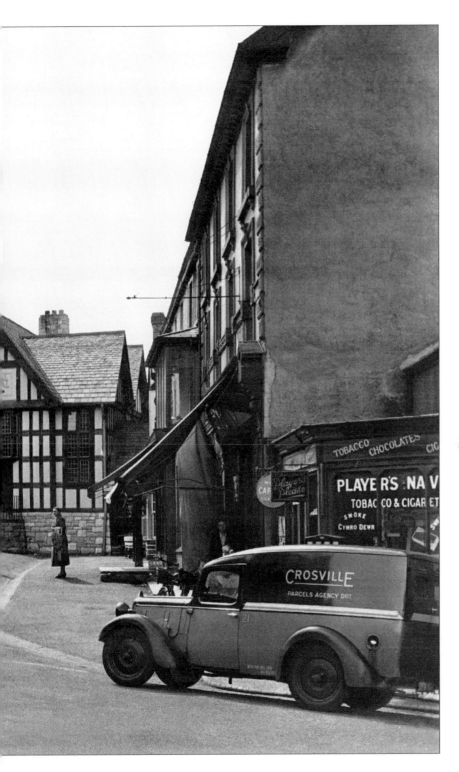

CORWEN
The Square c1950
C371035

Corwen has always been associated with Owain Glyndwr, self-proclaimed Welsh prince. The Glyndwr Hotel (left) speaks of the importance of his memory in this busy little town on the A5. The Crosville parcel van (right) obscures one of those quaint timber kiosks that are a rare survival today, but were always useful dispensers of tobacco, chocolate and reading matter.

▼ **CORWEN,** *From Flagstaff Hill c1965* C371067

This bird's eye view shows the railway north of Corwen and the A5 threading its way through the village - the road was to become the much busier of the two forms of transport. The church dominates the village. Corwen is one of the ancient parishes of Merioneth.

► **MAERDY**
The Goat Hotel c1960 M327006

The Goat was a smart traditional hotel on the A5 at the time of this photograph. Nowadays it is a busy corporate activity inn. The A5 is now much busier too.

◄ CLAWDD NEWYDD
The Village c1955
C368002

This marvellous view shows a local entrepreneur, W T Williams General Stores, supplying everything from fuel (at 1s 5d a gallon) to tea, and offering the usual local delivery service as well - note the van on the left.

► RUTHIN
St Peter's Square c1950
R292047

When Owain Glyndwr attacked the town in 1401, leaving little in his wake, it was one of many turbulent events in its history. The castle was commissioned by Edward I in 1277, and was later destroyed after an 11-week siege in 1646. Now it is popular with American visitors as an upmarket hotel. In this photograph, a 1930s coach waits while the driver chats with a priest, and we look past into the square. The timber-framed old courthouse of 1401 presses into the picture on the right.

▶ **RUTHIN**
The Castle c1960
R292084

The castle was originally ordered by Edward I, but it was finished in the custody of Reginald de Grey, Justiciar of Chester, in 1284. It was de Grey's descendents who provoked Glyndwr into rebellion just over 100 years later. The castle is now famous as an upmarket hotel specialising in medieval banquets.

◀ **RUTHIN**
Well Street c1960
R292107

The Hovis sign over the shop (left) would now be a collector's item, and so would the delivery van opposite. Further down the street the petrol pumps have gone, but cars are still sold from the garage.

▲ **RUTHIN,** *St Peter's Square c1965* R292164

A wonderfully varied street scene in this ancient town displays the varied architecture from different centuries in the town's history. Note the spire of the 1284 St Peter's Church, the monument, the much-loved 'eyes of Ruthin' (the prominent rows of dormer windows on the Myddleton Arms), and the Georgian Castle hotel (right). The last public execution, of Fr Charles Mahoney, took place here in 1679.

◀ **DENBIGH**
*The Castle, the Keep
1888* 20852

This impressive castle, again ordered by Edward I, was begun in 1283 and constructed on the site of the former Welsh stronghold of Dafydd ap Gryffudd. An English Borough that excluded the Welsh as residents was laid out also, and both Castle and Borough were enclosed within a protected town wall. The young lads watching in the distance appear to be in uniform - perhaps they are schoolboys.

DENBIGH
The Market Place 1888
20848

The deliberate poses of the onlookers ceases as we move into the 20th century. Fortunately for us, we can pore over their dress - and demeanour - in this image of Victorian Denbigh. The town has prospered from medieval times, and the market was vital in this growth. We can only imagine this concourse brimming with farmers, traders and livestock from those early days. Recent restoration works in the town are also revealing medieval buildings behind many of the seemingly later facades seen in this photograph.

59

▼ **DENBIGH,** *The Old Town Hall c1960* D22131

First erected in 1572, and remodelled in 1780, this fine public building continues its civic duties today as a library and museum.

► **DENBIGH**
High Street c1955
D22096

The contrasting styles of urban architecture seen in Denbigh speaks of its history and its regenerative powers, where medieval and Jacobean frontages are replaced with Georgian and Victorian modernisations. The parking arrangements would appear interesting today.

◄ **DENBIGH**
Howell's School
c1875 7701

The young girls we see climbing over the stile (right) suggest a more carefree time than we live in, and the scene is almost bucolic. The school was founded in 1859 by the trustees of Thomas Howell, a cloth merchant, who left a legacy of 12,000 gold ducats for the 'education of orphaned Welsh maidens'. This is obviously not a requirement to enter the school today, but the annual income from this legacy is still used to support some 'orphan scholars'.

► **DENBIGH**
The Cock Pit, the Hawk and Buckle Inn c1955
D22120

Cockfighting was a very popular pastime in rural Wales until its prohibition in 1849. Cocks would be pitched against each other and fought to the death, accompanied by much raucous gambling. This old cockpit, built in the 17th century, survives in the Museum of Welsh Life at St Fagan's near Cardiff - the cockpit was moved there and re-constructed in 1970. Derelict by 1965, it was latterly used as a slaughterhouse and a garage.

◀ **BODFARI**
The Tea Gardens, the Ace of Diamonds c1936 B461001

Attentive service is provided at this seemingly exclusive establishment with the racy name!

◄ BODFARI
The Dinorben Arms and the Church c1960 B461040

The church of St Stephen is thought to date originally from the 7th century; it is certainly recorded in a taxation document of 1254 as the church of 'Bottewara'. The church is much altered, and the earliest part surviving is the late medieval tower. The church and the rather later Dinorben Arms present a wonderfully sleepy picture in this village near St Asaph.

◄ HENLLAN
Llys Meirchion 1936 H288004

The name of this house, Llys, or court, of Meirchion, possibly indicates that this was the site of the home of Meirchion Gul, ancestor of St Winifride of Holywell fame. This much later building is the principal house in Henllan; here we see it standing rather sombrely waiting for some social occasion to bring it to life.

▶ **LLANFAIR TALHAIARN**
The Village c1955
L242041

Only minor changes would
be noticed in this small
village from the beginning
of the last century to this
day. The AA listed Black
Lion (left), like many other
inns at this time, helped
travellers by selling petrol
at the pump as well as beer.
The village is most revered
for having the grave of the
Welsh bard Taliesin.

◄ **GWYTHERIN**
The Post Office c1955
G168009

This sleepy row of terraced cottages has, in fact altered very little, although there is no longer a post office here. Seemingly miles from anywhere in the Denbighshire hinterland, Gwytherin still retains a pub, and it has managed to win Best Kept Village accolades in recent years. The village is famous for having the grave of St Winifride at Capel Gwenfrewi.

THE NORTH COAST - PRESTATYN TO LLANDUDNO

PRESTATYN, *The Promenade c1930* P110060

The cars and dress may be different, but a day by the sea changes little over the years. Here sun seekers sit or stroll on the promenade. Men's dress is still relatively formal, and the cars speak of some affluence. Yet in 1897, Dr Townsend, chairman of the local council, was concerned at the nature of public bathing and suggested the regulation of dress. He also suggested that 'bathing vans' be separated, and special concern was voiced about ladies 'undressing in the sand hills'.

PRESTATYN
High Street c1930
P110025

People walk in the roads, obviously unused to avoiding traffic - there is only a horse and cart and one small car in sight. The aptly named Palladium Café (right) seems a rather large establishment for the passing trade on view, and faces competition opposite from the Corner House Café.

PRESTATYN, *High Street c1950* P110089

Prestatyn can claim a history that is tangible from Roman times with its own Roman bath house. Before the Chester to Holyhead railway opened in the 19th century, Prestatyn relied on agriculture and various mining and quarrying activities. The railway also took labour away to work in the industries of Flintshire - and brought in large numbers of tourists. It is not a busy day in this photograph, and the shop awnings, deep shadows and the light summer dresses all suggest a very hot day in post-war Wales. The Palladium is immediately to the photographer's right.

PRESTATYN
High Street c1965
P110195

Looking in the opposite direction to photograph P110089 on page 67, we can see that the Palladium has now become a bingo hall (centre left) and that Dewhurst the butcher's has appeared as an infill development. There is much more bustle about this 1960s photograph, and a suggestion of easily accessible goods. The Fords and Vauxhall cars, and the TV rental shop Telefusion (beyond Dewhurst), testify to a growing prosperity as post-war austerity recedes further into memory. The refurbished Scala cinema opened in the town as the first arts centre of an Urban District Council in England and Wales.

◄ **TREMEIRCHION**
Rock Chapel
c1935 T182035

The Postal Directory of Flintshire, 1886, describes Tremeirchion as a 'considerable parish in the Vale of Clwyd'; near the Jesuit College of St Beuno stands a 'neat little chapel' on the hill, where 'a charming view of the country for many miles' can be enjoyed.

▲ **DYSERTH**
High Street c1955 D139082

Dyserth is most famous for its waterfall, attracting visitors in their hundreds. It is also rightly famous for being on the new (1905) branch line from Prestatyn, which was the first in North Wales to use the new motor train. One or two small coaches, with built-in steam engine, carried a recorded daily average of 450 passengers. The journey cost 3d.

RHYL, *Dyserth Falls c1940* R27116

Photographs of this waterfall vary so much from decade to decade that you could doubt they are one and the same location. They are a magnet for visitors to Dyserth. This particular picture reveals the cascade in all its glory, uncluttered by the trees that enclosed the fall in later years.

(Inset) **DYSERTH,** *The Waterfall 1891* 29162

▶ **RHUDDLAN**
The Castle 1891
29160

Like the bearskin helmets of guardsmen, these ivy-clad turrets still command respect over the surrounding countryside, much as they were intended to in 1277, when the castle was rebuilt for Edward I. It was a common sight at the time this photograph was taken to see our national monuments covered in ivy in this way.

◀ **RHUDDLAN**
Lower High Street 1951 R334021

On what is now Station Road, on the outskirts of the town, Marsh Hotel plied its trade in a position somewhat distant from the town. Two ladies chat in the porch, and the spaniel seems interested in the photographer in a scene virtually unaltered today.

▲ **RHUDDLAN,** *High Street 1935* R334024

Rhuddlan is most famous for its castle and its historic association with Edward I. There are remnants of medieval buildings in the town. For most of its history, though, it has had a quiet time, as we might guess from this photograph. A fine car approaches the High Street by the Parliament Building (right), and a dog feels safe enough to trot down the middle of the road. This would certainly be difficult to emulate today with the almost constant traffic on this road.

◄ **RHUDDLAN**
The Parliament Building c1940 R334026

This hybrid of a survival reveals in its stonework the continuing patchwork of alteration. A plaque tells us that a fragment remains of the house in which Edward I held his parliament and in which the Statute of Rhuddlan was passed in 1284, and in the gable end medieval windows are sealed with later stonework. The building was re-fashioned in the 18th and 19th centuries to what we see now.

◄ **ST ASAPH**
The Cathedral, the
West Front 1890 23297

The medieval cathedral
had been destroyed by the
armies of Henry III and
Edward I, and the present
building was rebuilt after
it was partially destroyed
by Owain Glyndwr in
1402. Even the Victorians
had their turn, with
Gilbert Scott remodelling
the unfortunate building
once again between 1867
and 1875.

◄ **ST ASAPH**
High Street c1960 S4050

This small city with a
population of 3,600 and
the smallest cathedral in
Britain has an important
place in the history of Wales.
Most notably, it was here
that William Morgan and a
number of helpers set about
the translation of the Bible
into the Welsh language, and
a memorial to those that
undertook this task stands
before the cathedral. The
town suffered repeatedly
through the Middle Ages, and
the cathedral was destroyed
on several occasions. The
scene here shows a quiet
provincial town. The postman
is perhaps finding the hill
difficult, and so is pushing
his bike up the hill. The
temporary No Parking signs
suggest that an event will be
under way at any time.

◄ **ST ASAPH**
Cefn Caves 1890 23303

A boy appears to be sitting for
the photographer, perhaps
wanting to lead him in to
reveal some of the caves'
secrets. The caves at Cefn
are amongst a number in
the Elwy Valley; they were
already famous in the 1530s,
when John Leland mentioned
them in his famous Itinerary
of 1536-39. Both animal and
human remains were found
in the first archaeological
examinations from the
1830s. In a cave nearby, at
Pontnewydd, remains were
found from the Neanderthal
period.

75

BODELWYDDAN, *The Church 1891* 29163

Bodelwyddan is rightly famous for 'the marble church' that stands proudly in the surrounding countryside near Rhuddlan, its spire reaching up 202 feet. It was erected in 1856-60 at a cost of £60,000 for Lady Willoughby de Broke as a memorial to her husband. The church was built in a variety of stone and marble, which gives it its more colloquial name. The picture shows the church 30 years old, pristine and splendid.

BODELWYDDAN
Lowther College c1950
B127028

The castle as we see it here was actually reconstructed between 1830 and 1852. Bodelwyddan Castle was the home of Lowther College, a leading public school for girls, for over sixty years from 1920 to 1982. Formed by Mrs Florence Lindley, Lowther College transferred to the castle, first as tenant and then purchasing the castle from the Williams family. The college run into financial difficulties and was forced to close in 1982. It is now a hotel, museum, art gallery and educational facility.

BODELWYDDAN, *The Wayside Café and Restaurant c1960* B127087

Resourceful individuals often took advantage of the growing number of visitors to North Wales in the post-war years. The Wayside, with its pretentious topiary garden, and trading in a residential setting, obviously hoped to satisfy some of this demand.

▼ **ST GEORGE,** *The Kinmel Arms c1960* S430025

The Austin 1100 sits proudly outside this 17th-century coaching inn near Abergele. It looks like a hot day, and a stop for light refreshment merely continues a centuries-old tradition dating here from the time of the Civil War. Perhaps some can just remember the time of this photograph, of being able to sit in a quiet, fairly plain bar with a glass of cold beer, with no machines, and no music. Halcyon days!

► **ST GEORGE**
Clarendon School c1960
S430031

Kinmel Hall stands on a site said to date back to 1311, but this present country house emerged from the ashes of a former mansion destroyed by fire in 1848. H R Hughes and the architect W E Nesfield built the present hall and gardens in the 1870s. This image shows the hall when it was used as a school between 1945 and 1975. In this last year it was again partially destroyed by fire. In recent years it has had a new lease of life as a hotel and conference centre.

◀ **RHYL**
The Victoria Pier and Pavilion 1892
30367

There were six piers in North Wales by 1900, and Rhyl was the second, opening in 1867. All manner of entertainment was provided in these extravagant buildings, from concerts and plays to minstrels and small 'sketches', and huge numbers would attend. By 1913 this grand building was replaced by a rather less ambitious single-storey amphitheatre. The pier fell into great disrepair, and was finally demolished in 1977.

▶ **RHYL**
East Parade 1895
36627c

The Conwy Memorial Fountain and garden beds that extend beyond into the distance lend an enticing elegance to the promenade that is now given over to a modern road and heavy traffic.

▶ RHYL
The Sands c1920
R27045

Donkey rides, beach chairs, heavy clothes - these are the delights of a British seaside day out! The Pavilion in the background provided further entertainment for the large audiences that attended in their thousands.

◀ RHYL
The Paddling Pool and the Pavilion c1955 R27273

The Pavilion, built in 1906 at a time when the North Wales resorts sought to improve their entertainment facilities, has become a firm Rhyl favourite over the years. The paddling pool is a precursor of the modern day Sun Centre, perhaps?

▲ **KINMEL BAY,** *Aled Gardens, Sandy Cove c1950* K112023

Well tended chalet gardens invite their occupants to sit outside and take in the sea air, obviously unpolluted by the fumes of heavy traffic.

◄ **KINMEL BAY**
Sandy Cove c1955
K112088

The new housing developments of both pre- and post-war Britain most often came with a small parade of shops to serve the new residents. Here, recently-built chalets shelter residents and visitors to the beaches, and these shops sold all the requisites, from groceries to postcards, to satisfy their needs.

TOWYN
Winkups Camp
c1955 T181061

The ability of some landowners to capitalise on the demand for cheap accommodation after the war led to a large number of caravan sites, such as Winkups, springing up around the Welsh coast, as elsewhere in Britain; this was before planning laws would seek to limit their growth as some sites became extensive.

ABERGELE, *Market Street 1890* 23331

By the date of this photograph, much of the town's main streets were established, and they display the characteristic detail of the period: projecting shop fronts proudly display their goods (including bales of cloth and blankets, left), and the dog has time to laze idly in the road!

RHYD-Y-FOEL
The Village c1955
R289057

Set below Pen y Corddyn Mawr, a Romano-British hill fort, these houses and cottages are a more recent addition to the ancient landscape of the North Wales coast.

LLANDULAS, *The Fair View Inn 1957* L69119

In the late fifties, the offerings over the bar were much fewer than today. Here we might think that Double Diamond was this pub's major selling point, as two passers-by are perhaps tempted in for a drink on this sunny-looking day.

83

OLD COLWYN
*The Wheelwright's
Shop 1890* 23356

The wheelwright in Old
Colwyn was always busy
making and repairing
wheels and carts, as an
inspection of the picture
reveals. A number of new
wheels are ready for fitting,
planks of new timber wait
to be used, and the men
come and pose. There
was probably always an
inquisitive audience for
such work.

▼ **OLD COLWYN** *1890* 23354

With the faded lime wash and rough appearance of the cottages and walls, this scene has an almost Mediterranean air about it. The maids seem to find the visitor ready for a chat, and the lad on the carriage looks back also.

► **COLWYN BAY**
Bryn Euryn Quarry
1890 23373

Bryn Euryn, below which this limestone quarry once operated, has associations with an early hill fort, Roman remains and a nearby ruined late medieval mansion now known as Llys Euryn. These all make this an interesting place to explore.

◄ **COLWYN BAY**
The New Promenade 1897
40031

Extensive and beautiful sandy beaches brought ever-increasing numbers of visitors to the North Wales coast. The civic fashion was to lay down long promenades, like this one at Colwyn Bay, to allow the leisured classes to promenade and take their sea air without having to trudge through sand or pebbles.

► **COLWYN BAY**
General View 1898
42368

This general view looks west over the bay towards the town. Beyond the pier, which appears to be under construction, is Bryn Euryn, and Little Orme Head is in the distance (right). The housing that can be seen in the foreground is recent, and shows the development that Colwyn Bay's growing popularity as a resort was bringing to the area beyond the town.

COLWYN BAY
General View c1955
C141002

Viewed from the direction of Bryn Euryn, the prominence of the Victoria Pier is clear; Colwyn Bay sought to rival nearby Llandudno as the main attraction, as post-war mass tourism brought holidays to the ordinary family.

COLWYN BAY, *The Beach and the Pier c1950* C141013

The summer exodus of holidaymakers to the seaside resorts of Britain made piers a popular and lucrative venture. This Victoria Pier has had a chequered history. Opened in 1900, it was almost destroyed by fire in 1923 and 1933, but it was rebuilt on both occasions. The Pavilion could seat 2,500 for its popular entertainment. The 1950s was its swansong: it closed in 1958, then reopened as a disco, but finally closed in 1991.

COLWYN BAY, *Near Victoria Pier c1930* C141014

▶ **RHOS-ON-SEA**
The Promenade
1921 70795

In contrast to the impressively wide and well-built promenades to be seen in Llandudno and elsewhere, the fallen rubble wall on the left here and the submerged groynes give the impression of a less well-organised resort. The parked prams and carefree strollers suggest that it is still much appreciated by local residents.

◀ **RHOS-ON-SEA**
The Promenade
c1955 R265071

It is a nice sunny day; there are people about, and there is time for a leisurely chat, while some seem interested in the beach just out of shot. Rhos, as it is known, is less commercialised than some of its neighbours, and remains a gentle mix of resort and rural seaside town. You could nip in for some chocolate at Millers (left) while stocking up with fishing bait at the shop next door.

▲ **LLANDRILLO YN RHOS,** *The Church 1890* 23367

This view towards the Little Orme is now almost completely covered with housing developments, so we can dwell on this rustic scene and imagine the odd visitor wandering along the road, or members of the congregation making their way to the church on a Sunday.

◄ **PENRHYN BAY**
The Village c1960
P321113

Marlon Brando stars in 'Mutiny on the Bounty' on the advertising board (left). The Mace corner shop, Little Orme Stores, has customers, but this site today is dominated by a large roundabout and garage beyond.

▼ **LLANDUDNO,** *The Pier 1890* 23250

Packing the hillside of Happy Valley above Llandudno, holidaymakers and residents alike enjoyed the views of the activity below them beside the recently constructed Victoria Pier. Little Orme stretches away in the distance. The town is a stereotype of the genteel middle-class British seaside town with its sweeping promenade, pier, grand hotels and public spaces. The whole town was conceived and planned by Lord Mostyn, the major estate holder in the region.

► **LLANDUDNO**
The Conwy Valley 1890
23266

Only a short distance from the vigorously booming Llandudno, this faded lime-washed farmhouse reminds us that earning a living in the less hospitable reaches of the valley was somewhat more difficult. To whom is the 'new milk' offered in this remote location?

◄ **LLANDUDNO**
The Parade 1895
36570

This is a marvellously evocative scene, with everything going on that one might expect in a seaside resort. The 90ft-wide promenade sweeps around to the pier, the Pavilion and the Grand Hotel. Bathing machines offer discreet changing for bathers, and a coach is loading passengers to explore the local attractions.

► **LLANDUDNO**
Happy Valley 1913
65713

Happy Valley was described as one of the best public parks or 'leisure grounds' in Britain, and was presented to the town by Lord Mostyn. It afforded views over the bay and mountains, and its grassy slopes encouraged people to sit and enjoy. This photograph catches a well-attended outside performance by minstrels in the exotically designed bandstand.

LLANDUDNO
The Tram Track
c1935 L71230

To exploit the tourist potential of the relatively inaccessible Great Orme, the tram line was opened in 1902. This picture shows it being drawn up the steep hill by its hidden cable system - the same design as that used in San Francisco.

LLANDUDNO, *The Hotel, Great Orme Summit c1960* L71712

The tram arrives from the town below; a modern Triumph Herald estate has joined the older cars here; and refreshment is available at the hotel. There are views all around, and it must have seemed like a perfect day out to holiday makers in those years just before foreign package holidays provided fierce competition to the British resort.

LLANFAIRFECHAN, CONWY AND THE SOUTH

LLANFAIRFECHAN, *The Sands 1890* 23212

Are the ladies conscious of the camera? This marvellous image encapsulates the changes taking place in Llanfairfechan and similar villages at this time. The more recent terraced buildings can be seen rising behind the few smaller cottages that remained when this photograph was taken. The beach vans indicate where the sands actually start!

▼ **LLANFAIRFECHAN,** *The Village 1891* 29476

Many of the buildings we see here had recently been built in the third and fourth quarters of the 19th century as the town grew on the prosperity brought to the locality by visitors.

► **LLANFAIRFECHAN**
Main Street 1908 60771

The cart makes its way up the street to unload round the corner. A small boy in uniform wanders towards us, and the shop fronts entice us to look closer to spot familiar goods.

LLANFAIRFECHAN
1908 60772

The town developed as a Victorian holiday resort, as many did on the North Wales Coast. This parade of shops, housed in a building displaying the influence of the eastern reaches of the British Empire, suggests a steady trade. There was a brief respite for the men unloading the cart, and the Refreshment Rooms enticed customers with its selection of eatables. Charles Fisher offered 'complete House Furnishings' and the fashionable linoleum.

PENMAENMAWR
The Sands 1887 19909

The prosperity of the North Wales coastline grew steadily during the 19th and early 20th centuries. At Penmaenmawr, this was due both to the influx of holidaymakers and to the extensive quarrying from the mountains in the background of this photograph. Large buildings, hotels and boarding houses were erected, while on the sands below bathing huts and several frames of swings may be seen to the left.

▼ **PENMAENMAWR,** *General View 1892* 30328

The majestic sweep of the fertile fields down to the coast is also marked by the workings and spoils of man's need for the stone that is quarried from the mountain on this stretch of the coast. Penmaenmawr is pinned to the coast below the two peaks of Penmaenmawr and Penmaenbach. Tunnels were pierced though these peaks for the railway, and in later years a road tunnel was also blasted through.

► **PENMAENMAWR**
From the Hotel 1897
40037

This scene nowadays would be dominated by the A55 Expressway, but only a little over a hundred years ago many of the buildings in this photograph would only have recently been erected, built on the strength of the quarries and the new tourism.

◄ **DWYGYFYLCHI**
1915 65681

The sightseers on the coach arriving at the hotel reveal that the village was a 'must see' for visitors. It was the gateway to the Sychnant Pass, the mountain road to Conwy and the Fairy Glen. The table on the right is laid out with refreshments.

► **CONWY**
Castle Street 1913 65752

Built by Edward I, Conwy Castle glowers at the head of this street scene as it dominates the town. The building on the right is Aberconwy House, a rare survival of medieval Conwy and one of the oldest buildings in Wales. It was used as a temperance house around the time of the photograph. It is interesting that the half-timbering is contemporary with the picture, and conceals the original structure (which has now been restored by the National Trust).

CONWY
The Oldest House c1955 C156275

Here we see Aberconwy House some years after photograph 65752 was taken. For long described as 'the oldest house in Wales', and dating from the 1300s, this medieval merchant's house has attracted visitors since the early years of the last century. Here the black timber framing has been painted over in a facelift that is more suggestive of the appearance of the original.

CONWY, *The Castle 1913* 65753

Conwy Castle is the most impressive of the ring of castles built by Edward I. Here two smart cars and a chauffeur wait while their inquisitive passengers make off to explore this magnificent ruin. The castle was completed in 1287 after just four years. It is surprising that the castle had a garrison of just 30 men during much of its active life.

CONWY
The Castle 1890 26794

From whichever angle Conwy Castle is viewed, it dominates the scene. Even the relatively modern masonry supporting Telford's 1826 steel suspension bridge seems to pay homage to the medieval structure. The bridge was built after an accident on Christmas Day in 1806 when the ferry that normally carried people across the river turned over. Only two of the fifteen people aboard were saved.

CONWY, *Plas Mawr, the Reception Room 1898* 42009

Robert Wynn was a prominent gentleman and merchant, and his house displayed all the good taste that would be expected of a man of such standing. The fine plasterwork is a particularly notable survival.

◄ **CONWY**
Plas Mawr 1892 30343

Rivalling the castle in impressiveness, albeit on a lesser scale, is the Elizabethan town house of Robert Wynn, built between 1576 and 1585. In this photograph, taken when the building belonged to the Royal Cambrian Academy of Art, the stone mullioned windows and the craggy rough facade gave no indication of its former glory. The building has recently been restored, and now has a complete coat of lime plaster. If the castle is examined closely, the remnants of a plaster coat can also be discerned.

◄ **CONWY**
The Tubular Steel Railway Bridge 1898
42386

Conwy was already something of a tourist attraction by 1898 with its castle and remnants of the planned medieval town. The relatively more recent tubular steel railway bridge, built by Robert Stephenson in 1850, with stone towers sympathetic to the castle's appearance, is a modern reminder of the continuing importance of the town as a point to cross the River Conwy.

CONWY, *Plas Mawr, the Banqueting Hall 1898* 42012

A fine and impressive hall was an essential requirement of any man of standing, and Robert Wynn was no different in wishing to impress his visitors. Wynn's hall is the first room that his guests would reach once they had come through the entrance. Again, the plasterwork is of the highest craftsmanship, particularly around the fireplace, and the walls were lined with oak wainscotting.

◄ **CONWY**
The Smallest House in Great Britain 1933 85700

This curious little extension to one of the town wall towers is even more interesting because of the modern and incongruous-looking brick wall that looks as if it has just been built. The house, which measures 10 x 6 feet, has two rooms, and was once occupied by a rather tall man of 6ft 3ins! The wall has since been removed.

CONWY
*High Street and the
Castle Hotel c1955*
C156266

As the High Street runs down toward the medieval town wall gate and through to the harbour, the influence of Robert Wynn's Plas Mawr can be seen in the transomed stone mullions of the Castle Hotel and the stepped gables of the building on the left; both are of much later date, of course, but redolent of his own fine house.

CONWY, *The Harbour c1955* C156333

These fishing boats obviously still offered their owners a living. Today, Conwy is most famous for its mussels, pulled from the mussel beds in the Menai Straits. Pleasure craft in the background are the future of small fishing ports such as this.

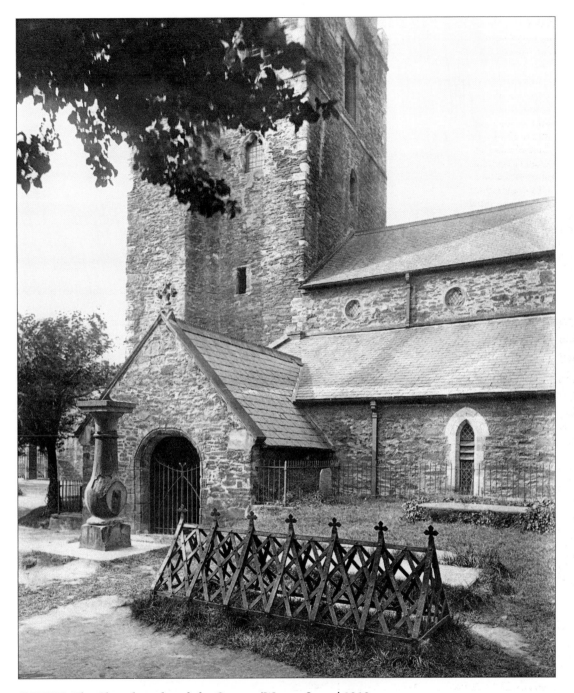

CONWY, *The Churchyard and the Grave - 'We are Seven' 1913* 65764

The church forms part of a Cistercian abbey founded in 1184, of which little remains. This photograph shows the remnants of an old grave, protected by ironwork, which is said to cover the remains of the small girl associated with Wordsworth's poem 'We are Seven'.

► **CONWY**
The Camp and Deganwy 1908
60746

North Wales has been a popular venue for the annual army camps for regulars and for the Territorial Army from around the turn of the 20th century. Training and the demands of foreign expeditions and wars, such as the Boer War of 1899-1902 and the Great War, required that the military maintained their preparations and helped in the necessary team building that produced good morale.

◄ **DEGANWY**
The Waterfront 1898
41481

This picture shows Deganwy before it had pretensions of being a resort. The few houses that have frontage to the river would never have anticipated the growth of residential building that would later take place here.

▲ **RO-WEN,** *The Village c1960* R346026

Apart from the electricity poles, the only clues to this scene being in the 20th century are the ubiquitous signs for Walls, Brooke Bond Tea and Woodbines, which probably now stir many an early memory.

◄ **DOLGARROG**
The Village c1955
D186013

Thirty years before this photograph was taken, the village had been devastated by a dreadful flood when two dams, the Eigau and the Coedty, broke after a fortnight of torrential rain. Sixteen people lost their lives amidst the debris and boulders that were washed down with the flood water.

TREFRIW
Llyn Cowlyd c1950
T70213

The lonely grandeur of
the Snowdonia mountains
is emphasised in stark
monochrome in this lake
set high above the village
on the flank of the Conwy
Valley. Once a perfectly wild
lake, it was dammed at the
beginning of the last century,
and is now the deepest
reservoir in Snowdonia.

▶ **TREFRIW**
The Village c1955
T70041

Trefriw, like so many Welsh villages, boasts a long history which is not always evident from the predominantly 19th-century buildings. It is now best known for its woollen mill, a magnet for tourists. Yet the quality of its spring water attracted great Roman interest, and the Trefriw Wells offered recuperative bathing facilities through to Victorian times, and are still a lure for visitors. The Fairy Falls Hotel was one of many built to welcome the leisured classes.

◀ **LLANRWST**
Y Bont Fawr and the Victoria Hotel 1892 30143

This beautifully proportioned stone bridge (Y Bont Fawr means 'the big bridge'), built over the Afon Conwy in 1636, has been a well-known beauty spot and subject for artists for centuries. The imposing Victoria Hotel shows the popularity of the Conwy Valley with Victorian tourists, who visited the town by coach, char-a-banc and train. The cart tracks in the foreground show a more humble mode of travel used by locals. The town also had a thriving wool, malting and tannery trade.

▲ **LLANRWST,** *Gwydyr Castle 1895* 36914

The fortified manor of the Wynn family, built at various stages from around 1490, is seen with carefully tended beds and wisteria and ivy-clad walls. Along with the magnificent town house of Plas Mawr in Conwy, they illustrate the dominance of this family in this region over many centuries. Shortly after this photograph was taken, in 1899, the future George V stayed here; part of the castle was destroyed by fire in the 1920s.

◄ **BETWYS-Y-COED**
The Miners Bridge 1891
29518

This wooden bridge was built over the River Llugwy so that the miners living in the village of Pentre Du could get to the lead mines of the Gwydir Forest. With the river at its torrential worst, it would still have been a difficult crossing without the bridge.

◄ **CAPEL CURIG**
*The Tan y Bwlch
Hotel 1891* 29536

Improved transport
opened much of North
Wales to the leisured
classes, who were able
to visit its grand and
picturesque scenery,
even in wilder and more
remote locations. The
hotel pictured here
offered comfortable
accommodation, and
this intrepid fisherman
is obviously hoping for a
prize fish to take his lure.

◄ BETWYS-Y-COED
Waterloo Bridge 1892
30103

There was little going on in Betwys-y -Coed until the road was improved for the Irish Mail in 1808. As part of the A5 road construction, Thomas Telford built the elegant Waterloo Bridge (Y Bont Haearn - the Iron Bridge) in 1815, and the defeat of Napoleon is proudly commemorated on its side.

◄ CAPEL CURIG
Plas Y Brenin c1960
C21034A

This wonderfully grand vista with Snowdon in the background is one of the most photographed and painted views in Snowdonia. The Plas y Brenin Outdoor Pursuits Centre, converted from the King's Hotel in 1954 to provide excellence in outdoor pursuit training, is seen in the middle distance.

DOLWYDDELAN
*The Bridge and the
Lledr c1940* D187011

The photographer
must have felt far from
the rumblings of war,
and even more so with
subjects as beautiful as
this fine old stone bridge
that spans the Lledr
River.

DOLWYDDELAN, *The Castle 1891* 29541

The rocky approach to this prominent outcrop upon which stands the small tower and remains of a larger castle looks wild, lonely and romantic, and it must have seemed a solitary outpost at times. It was built by Llewelyn the Great between c1210 and 1240, but it fell to Edward I in 1283, who then strengthened the fortress as part of his own defences.

INDEX

The Francis Frith Collection Titles

www.francisfrith.com

The Francis Frith Collection publishes over 100 new titles each year. A selection of those currently available is listed below. For the latest catalogue please contact The Francis Frith Collection.

Town Books 96 pages, approximately 75 photos. **County and Themed Books** 128 pages, approximately 135 photos (unless specified). Pocket Albums are miniature editions of Frith local history books 128 pages, approximately 95 photos.

Accrington Old and New
Alderley Edge and Wilmslow
Amersham, Chesham and Rickmansworth
Andover
Around Abergavenny
Around Alton
Aylesbury
Barnstaple
Bedford
Bedfordshire
Berkshire Living Memories
Berkshire Pocket Album
Blackpool Pocket Album
Bognor Regis
Bournemouth
Bradford
Bridgend
Bridport
Brighton and Hove
Bristol
Buckinghamshire
Calne Living Memories
Camberley Pocket Album
Canterbury Cathedral
Cardiff Old and New
Chatham and the Medway Towns
Chelmsford
Chepstow Then and Now
Cheshire
Cheshire Living Memories
Chester
Chesterfield
Chigwell
Christchurch
Churches of East Cornwall
Clevedon
Clitheroe
Corby Living Memories
Cornish Coast
Cornwall Living Memories
Cotswold Living Memories
Cotswold Pocket Album
Coulsdon, Chipstead and Woodmanstern
County Durham
Cromer, Sheringham and Holt
Dartmoor Pocket Album
Derby
Derbyshire
Derbyshire Living Memories
Devon
Devon Churches
Dorchester

Dorset Coast Pocket Album
Dorset Living Memories
Dorset Villages
Down the Dart
Down the Severn
Down the Thames
Dunmow, Thaxted and Finchingfield
Durham
East Anglia Pocket Album
East Devon
East Grinstead
Edinburgh
Ely and The Fens
Essex Pocket Album
Essex Second Selection
Essex: The London Boroughs
Exeter
Exmoor
Falmouth
Farnborough, Fleet and Aldershot
Folkestone
Frome
Furness and Cartmel Peninsulas
Glamorgan
Glasgow
Glastonbury
Gloucester
Gloucestershire
Greater Manchester
Guildford
Hailsham
Hampshire
Harrogate
Hastings and Bexhill
Haywards Heath Living Memories
Heads of the Valleys
Heart of Lancashire Pocket Album
Helston
Herefordshire
Horsham
Humberside Pocket Album
Huntingdon, St Neots and St Ives
Hythe, Romney Marsh and Ashford
Ilfracombe
Ipswich Pocket Album
Isle of Wight
Isle of Wight Living Memories
King's Lynn
Kingston upon Thames
Lake District Pocket Album
Lancashire Living Memories
Lancashire Villages

Available from your local bookshop or from the publisher

The Francis Frith Collection Titles (continued)

Lancaster, Morecambe and Heysham Pocket Album
Leeds Pocket Album
Leicester
Leicestershire
Lincolnshire Living Memoires
Lincolnshire Pocket Album
Liverpool and Merseyside
London Pocket Album
Ludlow
Maidenhead
Maidstone
Malmesbury
Manchester Pocket Album
Marlborough
Matlock
Merseyside Living Memories
Nantwich and Crewe
New Forest
Newbury Living Memories
Newquay to St Ives
North Devon Living Memories
North London
North Wales
North Yorkshire
Northamptonshire
Northumberland
Northwich
Nottingham
Nottinghamshire Pocket Album
Oakham
Odiham Then and Now
Oxford Pocket Album
Oxfordshire
Padstow
Pembrokeshire
Penzance
Petersfield Then and Now
Plymouth
Poole and Sandbanks
Preston Pocket Album
Ramsgate Old and New
Reading Pocket Album
Redditch Living Memories
Redhill to Reigate
Richmond
Ringwood
Rochdale
Romford Pocket Album
Salisbury Pocket Album
Scotland
Scottish Castles
Sevenoaks and Tonbridge
Sheffield and South Yorkshire Pocket Album
Shropshire
Somerset
South Devon Coast
South Devon Living Memories
South East London
Southampton Pocket Album
Southend Pocket Album

Southport
Southwold to Aldeburgh
Stourbridge Living Memories
Stratford upon Avon
Stroud
Suffolk
Suffolk Pocket Album
Surrey Living Memories
Sussex
Sutton
Swanage and Purbeck
Swansea Pocket Album
Swindon Living Memories
Taunton
Teignmouth
Tenby and Saundersfoot
Tiverton
Torbay
Truro
Uppingham
Villages of Kent
Villages of Surrey
Villages of Sussex Pocket Album
Wakefield and the Five Towns Living Memories
Warrington
Warwick
Warwickshire Pocket Album
Wellingborough Living Memories
Wells
Welsh Castles
West Midlands Pocket Album
West Wiltshire Towns
West Yorkshire
Weston-super-Mare
Weymouth
Widnes and Runcorn
Wiltshire Churches
Wiltshire Living Memories
Wiltshire Pocket Album
Wimborne
Winchester Pocket Album
Windermere
Windsor
Wirral
Wokingham and Bracknell
Woodbridge
Worcester
Worcestershire
Worcestershire Living Memories
Wyre Forest
York Pocket Album
Yorkshire
Yorkshire Coastal Memories
Yorkshire Dales
Yorkshire Revisited

See Frith books on the internet at www.francisfrith.com

FRITH PRODUCTS & SERVICES

Francis Frith would doubtless be pleased to know that the pioneering publishing venture he started in 1860 still continues today. Over a hundred and forty years later, The Francis Frith Collection continues in the same innovative tradition and is now one of the foremost publishers of vintage photographs in the world. Some of the current activities include:

Interior Decoration

Today Frith's photographs can be seen framed and as giant wall murals in thousands of pubs, restaurants, hotels, banks, retail stores and other public buildings throughout the country. In every case they enhance the unique local atmosphere of the places they depict and provide reminders of gentler days in an increasingly busy and frenetic world.

Product Promotions

Frith products are used by many major companies to promote the sales of their own products or to reinforce their own history and heritage. Frith promotions have been used by Hovis bread, Courage beers, Scots Porage Oats, Colman's mustard, Cadbury's foods, Mellow Birds coffee, Dunhill pipe tobacco, Guinness, and Bulmer's Cider.

Genealogy and Family History

As the interest in family history and roots grows world-wide, more and more people are turning to Frith's photographs of Great Britain for images of the towns, villages and streets where their ancestors lived; and, of course, photographs of the churches and chapels where their ancestors were christened, married and buried are an essential part of every genealogy tree and family album.

Frith Products

All Frith photographs are available Framed or just as Mounted Prints and Posters (size 23 x 16 inches). These may be ordered from the address below. From time to time other products - Address Books, Calendars, Table Mats, etc - are available.

The Internet

Already ninety thousand Frith photographs can be viewed and purchased on the internet through the Frith websites and a myriad of partner sites.

For more detailed information on Frith companies and products, look at this site:

www.francisfrith.com

See the complete list of Frith Books at:
www.francisfrith.com
This web site is regularly updated with the latest list of publications from The Francis Frith Collection. If you wish to buy books relating to another part of the country that your local bookshop does not stock, you may purchase on-line.

For further information, trade, or author enquiries please contact us at the address below:
The Francis Frith Collection, Frith's Barn, Teffont, Salisbury, Wiltshire, England SP3 5QP.
Tel: +44 (0)1722 716 376 Fax: +44 (0)1722 716 881 Email: sales@francisfrith.co.uk

See Frith books on the internet at www.francisfrith.com

FREE PRINT OF YOUR CHOICE

Mounted Print
Overall size 14 x 11 inches (355 x 280mm)

Choose any Frith photograph in this book.
Simply complete the Voucher opposite and return it with your remittance for £3.50 (to cover postage and handling) and we will print the photograph of your choice in SEPIA (size 11 x 8 inches) and supply it in a cream mount with a burgundy rule line (overall size 14 x 11 inches).
Please note: photographs with a reference number starting with a "Z" are not Frith photographs and cannot be supplied under this offer.
Offer valid for delivery to one UK address only.

PLUS: Order additional Mounted Prints at HALF PRICE - £8.50 each (normally £17.00)
If you would like to order more Frith prints from this book, possibly as gifts for friends and family, you can buy them at half price (with no additional postage and handling costs).

PLUS: Have your Mounted Prints framed
For an extra £17.00 per print you can have your mounted print(s) framed in an elegant polished wood and gilt moulding, overall size 16 x 13 inches (no additional postage and handling required).

IMPORTANT!

These special prices are only available if you use this form to order. You must use the ORIGINAL VOUCHER on this page (no copies permitted). We can only despatch to one UK address. This offer cannot be combined with any other offer.

Send completed Voucher form to:
The Francis Frith Collection, Frith's Barn, Teffont, Salisbury, Wiltshire SP3 5QP

CHOOSE A PHOTOGRAPH FROM THIS BOOK

Voucher *for FREE and Reduced Price Frith Prints*

Please do not photocopy this voucher. Only the original is valid, so please fill it in, cut it out and return it to us with your order.

Picture ref no	Page no	Qty	Mounted @ £8.50	Framed + £17.00	Total Cost £
		1	Free of charge*	£	£
			£8.50	£	£
			£8.50	£	£
			£8.50	£	£
			£8.50	£	£
			£8.50	£	£

Please allow 28 days for delivery. Offer available to one UK address only

* Post & handling	£3.50
Total Order Cost	£

Title of this book . . . .
I enclose a cheque/postal order for £ . . . .
made payable to 'The Francis Frith Collection'

OR please debit my Mastercard / Visa / Maestro card, details below

Card Number

Issue No (Maestro only)   Valid from (Maestro)

Expires   Signature

Name Mr/Mrs/Ms . . . .
Address . . . .
. . . .
. . . .
. . . . Postcode . . . .
Daytime Tel No . . . .
Email . . . .

1-85937-826-9   Valid to 31/12/09

Can you help us with information about any of the Frith photographs in this book?

We are gradually compiling an historical record for each of the photographs in the Frith archive. It is always fascinating to find out the names of the people shown in the pictures, as well as insights into the shops, buildings and other features depicted.

If you recognize anyone in the photographs in this book, or if you have information not already included in the author's caption, visit the Frith website at: www.francisfrith.com and add your memories.

Our production team

Frith books are produced by a small dedicated team at offices in the converted Grade II listed 18th-century barn at Teffont near Salisbury, illustrated above. Most have worked with The Francis Frith Collection for many years. All have in common one quality: they have a passion for The Francis Frith Collection. The team is constantly expanding, but currently includes:

Andrew Alsop, Paul Baron, Jason Buck, John Buck, Jenny Coles, Heather Crisp, David Davies, Natalie Davis, Louis du Mont, Isobel Hall, Chris Hardwick, Neil Harvey, Julian Hight, Peter Horne, James Kinnear, Karen Kinnear, Tina Leary, Stuart Login, Sue Molloy, Sarah Roberts, Kate Rotondetto, Eliza Sackett, Terence Sackett, Sandra Sampson, Adrian Sanders, Sandra Sanger, Julia Skinner, Lewis Taylor, Will Tunnicliffe, David Turner and Ricky Williams.